BRITISH BUSES

OF THE 1980s

JOHN LAW

FONTHILL

The Leyland Lynx was a true product of the mid and late 1980s. Two examples are shown here. The top photo shows an example bought by Wrexham independent, Wright's. F259GWJ is seen in the town's bus station in August 1989. Below is E420EBH, belonging to Jubilee Coaches, photographed in Stevenage bus station, where it was a regular performer on competitive services in spring 1988.

Fonthill Media Limited
Fonthill Media LLC
www.fonthillmedia.com

First published in the United Kingdom 2014

British Library Cataloguing in Publication Data:
A catalogue record for this book is available from the British Library

Copyright © John Law 2014

ISBN 978-1-78155-227-8

Typeset in 9.5pt on 11pt Mrs Eaves Serif Narrow.
Printed and bound in England

connect with us
 facebook.com/fonthillmedia   twitter.com/fonthillmedia

Introduction

As I begin to write these words, I learn of the death of Baroness Margaret Thatcher, on the 8 April 2013. Whatever your thoughts and opinions about the 'Iron Lady' (I'll keep mine to myself), the fact remains that her Premiership saw some of the biggest changes in the bus industry throughout the 1980s. She remained in power for the entire decade, presiding over deregulation and privatisation of much of Britain's buses.

We will look at the above in a few moments, but first a few words about this book and the reasons for its production. Although I had been photographing buses since the 1960s, it was not until early 1980 that I ceased taking monochrome photographs and took only colour transparencies. At the time, I was working for British Rail, so getting around the country was not a great financial burden. Therefore I was able to photograph Britain's bus scene throughout the decade. Nearly all the photographs are from my own camera, the only exceptions being a few from my old friend Jim Sambrooks and one from Fife by Richard Huggins, as all my 1980s pictures there have been published in Walter Burt's excellent book on the subject.

Deregulation of the bus industry was one of the Conservative Government's key policies. The Transport Act 1980 enabled this to happen. The first part of the bus industry to be freed from its reins was the long distance express coach sector. National Express, then part of the National Bus Company, had long been the dominant English operator, but soon found themselves faced by competition by British Coachways. This was a consortium of well-established companies, including Wallace Arnold, Shearings and others, but did not last long, being disbanded in 1982.

Between 1981 and 1984, three trial areas of deregulated bus services were established. Most of these were in small, rural locations and made little difference to the provision of bus services to the villages served. Only one place of significance was affected, the small cathedral city of Hereford. Several small independents commenced competitive services here, but were soon vanquished to memories by the might of Midland Red and several other well-established operators. I visited Hereford in 1985 and managed to photograph the bus scene here, as you will see within these pages.

The Transport Act 1985 then brought full deregulation of stage carriage services on 26 October 1986. This applied throughout mainland Britain, except for Greater London. To this day, bus services in London are still regulated, nowadays under the auspices of Transport for London.

While all the above was happening, gradual changes took place within the nationalised section of the British bus industry. Many of the larger operations of the National Bus Company and Scottish Bus Group were split into smaller concerns. For example, Midland Red was sectioned into four, Midland Fox, Midland Red North, Midland Red South and Midland Red West. In Scotland new SBG operators emerged, Strathtay and Clydeside. All this was done to assist the sale of all NBC and SBG companies. All English companies had been sold by 1989, with Scotland following early in the next decade. Meanwhile corporate colour schemes began to be replaced by new liveries.

Most of the existing council or Passenger Transport Executive bus operations remained basically unchanged during the 1980s, though they too were being prepared for privatisation or 'arm's length' control.

A notable sale, in 1985, was that of Burton-on-Trent's buses (operated by East Staffordshire District Council) to local independent Stevensons of Spath.

The Government's policies also brought great changes to Britain's smaller operators. The early part of the decade saw several companies being bought out by larger neighbours, but deregulation in 1986 meant that commercial bus routes could be started by any company, with only fifty-six days' notice of commencement, or withdrawal. Many small independent companies, previously confined to private hire and contract operations, decided to enter the fray, competing with the resident major operator. Bus wars broke out in several places, some of them being in quite unlikely locations. Market forces prevailed, of course, and the stronger concern usually won, or bought out the independent.

Loss making services, deemed socially necessary by local government, were subsided and put out to tender. Independent operators won many of these, adding variety for bus enthusiasts like me.

In the early 1980s, with deregulation and privatisation looming, many people predicted dire consequences for the bus industry. Hindsight has shown us that these didn't happen, of course. However, there was one event that I, plus many others, did not foresee - the minibus revolution. In preparation for expected competition, many operators bought fleets of tiny minibuses, mainly Ford Transit or Freight Rover Sherpa van conversions. Places like Oxford and Exeter soon became awash with the damned things! Nevertheless, the tactic proved effective, deterring the competition. By the later part of the decade, the Transits and Sherpas were being replaced by larger and more suitable vehicles, such as the Mercedes 709D or Optare's City Pacer and StarRider midibuses.

Despite the influx on smaller machines, development of normal size buses continued. Leyland Motors, with its Atlantean double decker, Leopard saloon and National integral, were well established as the eighties began. The Atlantean ceased production in 1984, being replaced by the Olympian. Similarly construction of the Leopard chassis stopped in the early 1980s, with its bus replacement being the Lynx and the Tiger. With the demise of the National Bus Company came the death of the Leyland National, the last ones hitting the road in 1985. March 1988 saw Leyland being taken over by Volvo.

Of course, Leyland did not have the bus market to itself. MCW, with its Metrobus double decker, supplied many operators, though this ceased production in 1989. Dennis, a specialist vehicle manufacturer in Surrey, re-entered the bus market in the late 1970s, selling it Dominator 'decker right through the eighties.

The above is not meant to be a thorough list of bus manufacturers throughout the 1980. Others include Volvo, Scania, Bedford and Ford. I've tried to include a good variety of these within these pages and hopefully I've captured the essence of the 1980s bus world as well. Being just a snapshot of the decade, it has proved impossible to show every vehicle type of location. If your favourite bus, operator or town isn't included, please accept my apologies. I could not be everywhere at once! However, I have more than enough photographs to fill another book, so watch out for a second volume.

Finally, my thanks to Richard Huggins, Jim Sambrooks, those marvellous people at Wikipedia and Bus Lists on the Web, plus Fonthill Media for assistance in the production of this book. I hope you enjoy it.

A look at Chepstow to start with. Despite long established policies of standardisation, the National Bus Company purchased several second hand vehicles in the early 1980s. National Welsh HR5467 (JKG477F), a Daimler Fleetline/MCW new to Cardiff City Transport is seen, proudly wearing NBC red livery at Chepstow bus station in mid 1980.

On the same day, National Welsh's Chepstow town service was being operated by this rare Leyland Redline with Asco 19 seat bodywork, a totally non-standard vehicle for an NBC fleet.

The Leyland Olympian was very much a product of the 1980s. A typical example is A140TPE, carrying Roe bodywork. It was new to London Country Bus Service as fleet number LR40. With privatisation it passed to Sovereign, inheritors of LCBS's North East area. It is seen in mid 1989, to the rear of Hatfield railway station, heading for Stevenage on the 300 route from Hemel Hempstead. Sovereign did not use fleet numbers.

A similar Olympian, albeit with ECW bodywork, is JTY376X, fleet number 3576 in the Northern General fleet, seen in Jarrow depot in spring 1984. Alongside is 3362 (DGR862S), a 1978 Bristol VR with rare Willowbrook bodywork.

Plymouth City Transport was, for many years, a stronghold of the Leyland Atlantean. On a rainy day in March 1981, two of the breed are seen in Plymouth's Bretonside bus station. 192 and 193 are 1965 examples of the PDR1/1 marque. Both carry standard Metro-Cammell bodywork. Both would be withdrawn shortly after being photographed.

In contrast to the above, fleet number 175, named 'Ark Royal', was almost new when photographed at the depot c. 1985. It is a coach seated Volvo Citybus with East Lancs bodywork.

In May 1986, United Automobile Services were preparing themselves for privatisation. This gave them the freedom to introduce new liveries, or, in this case, bring back an old one. The former coaching colour scheme is seen applied to open top Bristol RELL PHN178L. Normally engaged in sea front work, it's seen outside Grosmont station, operating a rail replacement service for the North Yorkshire Moors Railway.

Brand new at the time, we see the first of many minibuses within these pages. United's 2411 (C411VVN) was a standard Mercedes Benz L608D with 20 seat bodywork. It was photographed operating a Scarborough 'Skipper' local service. At the time, minibuses were being introduced nationwide, as a countermeasure against expected competition brought about by deregulation.

Hereford has long been a good place to find independent buses and coaches. As a trial area for deregulation, even more were to be found on the city's streets. Buchanans/Western Coaches, based at Stretton Sugwas, was one company to try out stage services during that period. WUG143S was a Bedford YMT carrying Duple Dominant coachwork, seen on bus duties in Hereford city centre during mid 1985. This was new to Hargreaves of Morley, Yorkshire, and later passed to Yeomans (see below).

Yeomans was, indeed still is, a long established bus operator in Hereford, serving both city and the surrounding countryside. A typical vehicle in the fleet of the 1980s was number 1, registered PGR619N. This Bedford YRQ/Willowbrook bus was new to North East independent, Jolly of South Hylton. I found it in Hereford bus station on a sunny day in mid 1989.

One of my favourite independent operators was OK Motor Services, based in Bishop Auckland and I make no apologies for showing two examples of the fleet here. In the summer of 1980, ex Glasgow Corporation KUS596E loads up in Bishop Auckland's Market Place. It is a Leyland Atlantean PDR1/1 with Alexander bodywork. Never the most convenient place for a bus terminus, services now use a purpose built bus station nearby.

A later OKMS Leyland Atlantean was XUP348L, an AN68 with Northern Counties body. New to the company in 1973, it is seen on service in West Auckland, again in the summer of 1980.

The London Transport DMS type Daimler/Leyland Fleetline did not find favour in the capital and the type was soon sold on to other operators, starting in 1979 and continuing through into the eighties. London's DMS2137 (OJD137R) was actually a Leyland built example, seen here in the hands of Grahams of Hawkhead, carrying fleet number D5. It was photographed in Paisley town centre in the summer of 1986. About to overtake is another London exile, AEC Routemaster WLT694, owned by Clydeside, a former Scottish Bus Group subsidiary, formed to take over part of the Western SMT empire.

Similar OJD192R (ex DMS2192) is seen on a foul summer day in 1984, in the city of Peterborough. It is owned by local independent Morley's and is heading for its home town of Whittlesey, pursued by an Eastern Counties Bristol RE.

London's tourist services were provided by a number of operators during the 1980s. In autumn 1987, Southend Transport supplied B555ATX, originally delivered as Cardiff Transport 555. It is a Leyland Olympian/East Lancs. Seen in Tooley Street, near London Bridge, it is operating at Culturebus service. It later returned to Cardiff.

Seen at its Victoria terminus some time around 1982, Alder Valley 985 (CJH125V) is specially painted in London Transport livery for sightseeing duties. This Bristol VRT/SL3/8LXB carries coach seated ECW bodywork.

The Bristol Omnibus Company was split up into various smaller concerns during the 1980s, as a prelude to privatisation. The photographs on this page were taken just before that period, during National Bus Company days. The classic style of ECW dual-purpose coachwork is seen here on fleet number 2441 (KHW315E) at Gloucester bus station in mid 1980. This Bristol RELH was new in July 1967.

A later single deck vehicle for Bristol Omnibus was number 3623 (BHY997V), a Series 2 type Leyland National, very much a standard NBC bus of the time. It is seen in central Swindon in 1982.

Cleveland Transit (previously known as Teesside Municipal Transport) came about after the amalgamation of Stockton & Middlesborough Corporation transport departments plus the Teesside Railless Traction Board. A mainly standardised fleet was owned, but this page shows a couple of rarer buses. Number 317 (HPY317N) is one of a pair of Ford A series minibuses with North Counties bodywork. It is seen in central Middlesborough in spring 1981.

Number 372 was even more unusual! KXG372L This was originally delivered as a Willowbrook Expressway bodied Leyland Leopard coach. Following a successful rebodying programme of a batch of Leyland Atlanteans, Cleveland Transit decided to do the same thing with this, designing the body themselves, though it was finished off by Northern Counties. I found it in Middlesborough's new bus station in mid 1988.

Competition came to the East Lancashire towns in the later years of the 1980s.Several coach companies started services around Blackburn and Accrington. In autumn 1988, Pilkington's of Accrington URR197G is seen on service in Blackburn bus station. It's a Bedford VAM/Plaxton Elite coach, not totally suitable for urban stage carriage work.

Still in all over white, a reminder of its National Express days is CUF261L. New to Southdown in 1973, it is a Leyland Leopard with Duple Dominant coachwork. It's seen here, in the hands of Accrington Coachways, in its home town, spring 1987. Again it is on local stage duties, heading for Blackburn.

Ulsterbus, with its virtual monopoly of bus services in Northern Ireland, managed to get through the 1980s without all the major changes of the mainland. Typical of the fleet was number 1671 (FOI1671), a Bristol LH6L/Alexander (Belfast) 45 seat bus, seen in Derry bus station *c.* 1982.

On the same visit across the Irish Sea, I found this 1961 built Leyland PD3/4 bodied by UTA, a training vehicle with Ulsterbus. No 846 (8846AZ) was found in central Belfast.

The outer reaches of the West Midlands feature on this page. This Mark II MCW Metrobus of Travel West Midlands was fitted with coach seating for use on the longer distance routes. 2947 (D947NDA) was found in Lichfield in spring 1987, not long after delivery in late 1986,

Like many operators, Travel West Midlands bought some Ford Transit minibuses. Seen amongst its larger compatriots is number 564 (B64AOP), photographed in Sutton Coldfield in spring 1987.

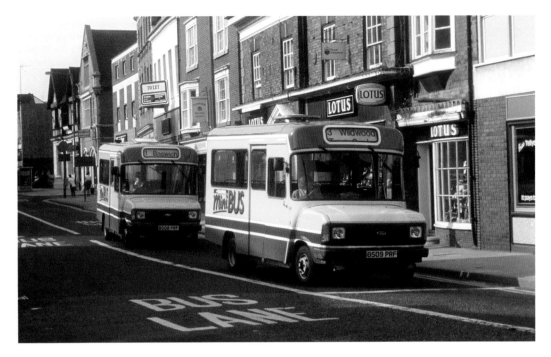

The minibus revolution brought two types of "breadvans" to the major fleets of Great Britain. Midland Red North's Ford Transits took over the streets of Stafford. A pair is seen here in 1985. Leading is number 9 (B509PRF), a 16 seat Dormobile conversion.

Competing with the Ford Transit was the Freight Rover Sherpa. This example, again bodied by Dormobile, is number 58 in the National Welsh fleet. I found it in Pontypridd in late 1986.

The sun does come out in the North East! Northern General; MCW Metrobus 3497 (DVK497W) arrives in Newcastle city centre in the spring of 1981, not long after delivery in October 1980. Prior to this date, the Metrobus was an unusual type for an NBC operator. .

A more standard bus in the Northern General fleet was 3428 (JPT928T), though this "highbridge" Bristol VRT/SL3/501 with ECW bodywork carried a decidedly non standard colour scheme. The blue and white livery was that of Sunderland District Tramways and it is appropriate that I photographed the bus, along with that young lady, in Sunderland town centre in September 1980.

The NBC's Bristol VR/ECW buses sometimes received non standard liveries. Alder Valley 981 (CJH1221V), a coach seated version, carries reversed NBC red and white, to designate its use on long distance duties. My old friend, the late Les Flint, took this photo for me at Reading in March 1981.

Fortunately Crosville, a former NBC subsidiary, did not apply this livery to the majority of its buses! Fleet number DVL443, registered RMA553V, was found in Stockport in spring 1987.

The Stockton area was a good place to find independent buses in the 1980s. Post deregulation, Delta of Thornaby began competing with the larger local concerns. Here, it's a gloomy spring day in 1987 and Delta's JEK68N is adding to the murk as it loads up in Stockton's wide High Street. The bus is a former Warrington Transport Bristol RESL bodied by East Lancs.

In the 1980s, Compass Royston of Stockton did not operate stage services, but their vehicles were often to be seen on schools and contract duties. In one of the town's housing estates, TRD709M is awaiting the last of its load of schoolchildren. This is quite an unusual vehicle, as it was formerly in the fleet of Alder Valley, an NBC subsidiary that rarely bought lightweight vehicles. It is an ECW bodied Ford R1014. At least it's a sunny day!

Interchange at Peterborough was possible between rail services and express coaches to Oundle, Corby and Kettering, At the latter terminus, interchange was again possible, with British Rail's Midland Main Line. United Counties operated the route, with dedicated vehicles painted in a BR style livery. Fleet number 243 (MRP243V), is a Leyland Leopard with 45 seat Plaxton Supreme coachwork, originally intended for Western National. This vehicle later saw service with Kelvin Central in Scotland. It's seen here at Peterborough station when newly delivered in 1980.

Later into the decade, another Rail Link was introduced from Peterborough, connecting the city with Wisbech, Kings Lynn and the coast at Hunstanton. Bird's Coaches of Hunstanton provided the vehicles, this one being painted in BR's latest "Inter City" colours. Photographed at Peterborough station in 1985, when almost new, it is a Ford R1115 with Plaxton Paramount 53 seat coachwork.

Minibuses proliferated in the Bristol and Somerset area in the 1980s. Bakers Dolphin Coaches, based at Weston-super-Mare, took on some tendered work in Bridgwater and it is on such duties that we see E522TOV at its town terminus in the summer of 1989. It is a Carlyle bodied Iveco 49.10, perfectly adequate for the job it was doing. By that time, minibuses had grown to increase capacity from the original Ford Transit 16 seaters.

Parked dubiously in Bristol city centre, in summer 1989, was this Optare City Pacer of Arrow Coaches. F936AWW was new to Arrow, despite the Yorkshire registration. It could be said that the City Pacer was the first purpose-built minibus, rather than a van conversion, with Optare using a Volkswagen LT55 chassis.

Leyland Atlanteans were still a common sight in the 1980s. A very late Atlantean was Barrow Transport's 105 (LEO736Y), an AN68D/1T delivered in February 1983. It carried Northern Counties 75 seat bodywork and is seen in Barrow-in-Furness town centre in mid 1983. This bus passed, along with the Barrow Borough Transport business, to Ribble in 1989.

Belfast Citybus 2891 (JOI2891) was a Leyland Atlantean AN68/2R with locally constructed Alexander bodywork, new in 1976. I photographed it in Belfast city centre on a nice sunny day, c. 1982.

Mulleys of Ixworth, Suffolk, had a wonderful selection of coaches during the 1980s. Seen at Angel Hill, its terminus in Bury St Edmunds, is XCV444, no doubt on some kind of stage service. This Bedford SB13/Duple C41F coach was typical of the fleet at the time, 1980.

In contrast to the above, WGV863X was a much more modern coach. Though it carries Mulleys lettering, the company had been taken over by Beeston's, another Suffolk operator. I found it under maintenance at Hadleigh depot in autumn 1983. New in 1982, it is a Duple bodied Leyland Leopard.

The northern section of United Automobile Services was to become Northumbria around 1986/7. Coach seated Leyland Olympian/ECW 264 (C265XEF) was new to United in May 1986. In view of the forthcoming changes, the vehicle was delivered in all-over white and I found it at Alnwick depot in June 1986.

Similar B248NVN, albeit with bus seats, was delivered to United as number 248. By the spring of 1987, when I photographed it in Newcastle city centre, it had become number 427 in the Northumbria fleet. Even on a dull Tyneside day the livery looks bright!

Central Coaches was the name of the coaching arm of Travel West Midlands. This Toyota midicoach, F955COJ, carries twenty seat Caetano coachwork and is seen in Newark bus station, Nottinghamshire, on a private hire in summer 1989.

For a short time, Central Coaches operated an express service to the capital, where London Transport's Victoria Garage provided stabling facilities. It's here, in spring 1986, that we see Bova Futura integral coach C903JOF, alongside a resident MCW Metrobus and AEC Routemaster.

South Wales was always host to a good number of independents. A long established one was S. A. Bebb, of Llantwit Fadre, who owned this Optare City Pace, E65SUH. A fine sunny day in mid 1989 found it on duty in Bridgend.

One of the best Welsh towns to see independent buses was Carmarthen. A larger concern serving here was Davies Bros of Pencader, who owned this former London Transport Bristol LH6L/ECW 39 seater, registered OJD53R. In June 1989, I found it in Carmarthen bus station, in advert livery, while alongside was HBX972X, a Bedford YNT/Duple bus owned by Jones of Login.

City of Oxford was the name of the NBC subsidiary serving the 'city of dreaming spires'. Prior to the mid 1980s, standard NBC red was employed and it is seen applied to fleet number 368 (WJN368J). This is an ex Southend Transport Daimler Fleetline/Northern Counties double decker, a most unusual bus to bear this colour scheme. I found it in Oxford city centre, near the 'Old Tom' bell tower, in early 1985.

Central Oxford's Bulldog pub makes a nice backdrop to City of Oxford 753 (E753VJO), an MCW Metrorider 25 seater, delivered in 1987. It was photographed in September of that year, in 'Nipper' green livery.

Devon General was once a bastion of AEC buses, but by the early 1980s, the most common double deck type was the Bristol VR/ECW. Bearing green paintwork (a sign of its Western National management) is number 1175 (FDV807V), seen in Exeter in March 1981.

By 1985, the minibus was beginning to dominate the Devon General fleet. Ford Transit number 22 (A268MTA) had bodywork completed by Midland Red. It is seen outside Exeter St Davids station in 1985. Plenty more were to come!

Eastern National were the proud owners of this unusual vehicle. Number 1404 in the fleet was a 1973 built Bristol RELH, hence the registration VHK177L. It later received a newer ECW coach body, as seen here near Wollaston, Northamptonshire, in 1982.

Eastern National ran into East London for many years, coming in from their home of Essex. The 1980s saw them win some tendered work wholly within Greater London. Seen in Romford in autumn 1985, heading for Walthamstow, is Leyland National 1801 (TJN500R). Signage on the bus clearly indicates that it is a London Transport service.

East Yorkshire Motor Services is a name that has continued from before the 1950s to the present day. Until the 1970s, the company's double deckers had specially profiled roofs to fit through the famous Beverley Bar. This is clearly seen on number 857 (NKH857F), a 1958 Daimler Fleetline with Park Royal bodywork. I photographed it in Hull, alongside Paragon railway station, in the summer of 1980.

Traditional EYMS livery is seen applied to a former London bus! Like many operators at the time, AEC Routemasters were bought and used on urban routes liable to suffer competition. Fleet number 802 (WLT798) was previously London Transport's RM798. Here, it is sitting in the sun, laying over in central Hull, in the summer of 1989.

Ipswich's Cattle Market bus station serves the Suffolk town's interurban and rural routes. It was here, in the spring of 1989, that I found GSX112N arriving. New to Lothian Transport, it was a Bedford YRT with classic Alexander Y type bodywork, seen in the hands of Blue Bus Services.

Another independent serving Ipswich was Bickers of Coddenham. A sunny day in 1985 saw RBD112M laying over in the Cattle Market bus station. This was another Bedford YRT, this time with Willowbrook bodywork. It was new to United Counties and later passed to Ipswich Borough Transport, along with the Bickers business.

The split up of London Country brought some new names and liveries to the towns around the capital. Two tone green and white was adopted by London Country North East, serving Hertfordshire and Essex. This livery is shown to good effect on fleet number SNB542 (EPD542V), a B type Leyland National, seen in Hemel Hempstead bus station in spring 1987.

London Country North West won some tendered work within Greater London. In October 1986, Mercedes L608D twenty seater number MBM10 (C310SPL) was photographed in the sun at Golders Green.

The Scottish Bus Group was to be privatised in the late 1980s and the early 1990s. Prior to those days, Fife Scottish had a virtual monopoly in its home territory and their red buses also left the Kingdom to Dundee, Glasgow and Edinburgh. An unusual vehicle was fleet number FRN8 (registration NRG156M), a former Grampian Leyland Atlantean AN68/1R with Alexander bodywork. It was photographed by Richard Huggins outside Cowdenbeath depot on the 20 May 1985.

The Scottish Bus Group was not immune to the trend towards smaller buses. Eastern Scottish took in some Dodge S56/Alexander minibuses. One of the batch was MR416 (D416ASF), seen in Edinburgh bus station in the summer of 1987.

The area around London's Victoria Station has long been good hunting round for bus enthusiasts. Tyne and Wear PTE's coaching business, Armstrong Galley, provided this fine double decker coach for me to photograph in mid 1987. Number 50 (A750CRG) is an MCW Metroliner, a relatively rare breed.

More or less at the same location and an even scarcer type of double decker. NVP533M started life as a Metro-Scania/MCW demonstrator, but is seen here on tourist duties with Rawson Brothers of Hayes, though it is in the livery of Globus Gateway. Wilton Street, Victoria, 1982.

Midland Red North ordered a small batch of Leyland Tiger buses, which were delivered in early 1984. Seen outside Shrewsbury depot is number 1702 (A702HVT), when only a few months old, in May 1984. Carrying Hotspur branding, it has Duple Dominant fifty-one seat bodywork and was intended for local services. Midland Red North had been formed in 1981 when the old Midland Red company had been divided into four. Evidence of the old owners can be seen on the depot wall.

Midland Red North later renamed itself as Midland Red, adopting a new livery. Bearing Chaserider Midland Red fleetnames, sister vehicle 1704 (A704HVT) was found in Tamworth in February 1989.

Eastern Counties Omnibus Company was the dominant NBC operator in Ipswich and here we see a standard Leyland National with the lower half extolling the virtues of joining the British Army. Fleet number LN783 (DPW783T) is seen in the Cattle Market bus station on a wet day in spring 1980, alongside ex Scottish Bus Group Bristol number VR332.

Bristol VRT/SL6G JNG50N started life with Eastern Counties in 1975 as a normal ECW bodied example, with a roof, and given fleet number VR152. How it managed to decapitate itself is not known, but it is seen here in Ipswich depot as number OT3 in 1986. At the time of writing, it still survives in preservation.

The City of Cardiff had been employing an orange livery for its council owned buses since the 1970s. This is seen to good effect on dual doored Leyland National 218 (JBO348N), having a well earned rest in the city centre in mid 1980.

Brand new at the time, early 1985, Cardiff City Transport number 559 (B559ARX) is a Leyland Olympian with East Lancs bodywork, photographed in Cardiff bus station. It is seen fitted with coach seating as it awaits departure for Tredegar on the long distance 36 route, a journey of a couple of hours. Anyone travelling the full length of the service would have appreciated the comfy seats!

PMT stood for Potteries Motor Traction, an NBC subsidiary serving that part of Staffordshire. Closest to the camera is fleet number 726 (NEH726W), a brand new Bristol VRT/SL2/501 with ECW bodywork. Production of the Bristol VR was to cease less than a year later. This bus was last reported as exported to Belgium. Similar, but slightly older, 704 is about to overtake in Longton bus station in the latter part of 1980.

The Bristol VR was superseded in part by the Leyland Olympian. Number 743 (A743JRE) in the PMT fleet is a typical example. Fitted with the usual style of ECW bodywork, it is seen departing Hanley bus station in 1985.

By June 1986, the expansion of the Stagecoach empire had begun. A long established independent, McLennan's of Spittalfield had recently been taken over and a visit to the depot proved fruitful for the camera. In a non standard livery was HDV639E, a 1967 Bristol MW6G/ ECW coach, new to Western National.

On the same occasion, this Bristol FLF6G/ECW decker is resplendent in Stagecoach stripes. KPW482E had started life with Eastern Counties as FLF482, but was soon sent to Eastern Scottish in exchange for a Bristol VR. After withdrawal by Stagecoach in 1991, it was exported to Canada and is now believed to be a static exhibit in Rochester, New York State, USA. Alongside is HSN656N, a Bedford YEQ/Plaxton coach, new to Watson of Dundee and still bearing McLennan's livery.

Stevensons of Spath (near Uttoxeter) was another bus company to expand rapidly in the 1980s. The company's original core route was from Uttoxeter to Burton-on-Trent and it is on that duty that we see number 18 (6MPT) in the fleet. New to Weardale Motor Services, this Plaxton bodied Leyland Leopard has since been preserved. Uttoxeter bus station, mid 1980.

In an unusual move, Stevensons took over a former municipal operator in 1985, with the purchase of the bus operations of East Staffordshire District Council. Previously known as Burton-on-Trent Corporation Transport, here we see number 10 (GFA19L) in that fleet, a Daimler Fleetline with Willowbrook bodywork to a design commissioned by Nottingham Transport. It is seen passing the old Burton bus station in 1982.

Crosville Motor Services purchased a large batch of Leyland Olympians, from 1982 onwards. Fleet number DOG173 (registered A173VFM) was a typical example, with seventy-seven seat ECW bodywork. It is seen, when almost new, on August bank holiday Sunday 1984, with a Snowdonian backdrop in Llanberis.

DOG194 (B194BLG) was a similar bus, delivered in 1985. When I photographed it in Shrewsbury, during the summer of 1987, it had gained the new colours of Crosville Cymru, after the original Crosville company had been split into Welsh and English operations. For those unfamiliar with the Crosville numbering system, "DOG" stood for Double decker, Olympian, Gardner engine.

East Midland Motor Services was one of the first former NBC operators to be bought by the Stagecoach Group. Prior to that, Leyland National 577 (OVO577M) is seen in the new livery adopted by EMMS from the previous NBC green. It is seen laying over at Doncaster's Southern bus station, on a sunny day in 1986.

Stagecoach livery has now been newly applied to East Midland Leyland Olympian/ECW 306 (SHE306Y), seen in the gloom of the Southern bus station, Doncaster, in autumn 1989.

Non red buses in London! Since the 1930s London's buses have been red, except for those in the former Country area, which were green. Londoners never knew that buses could ever be any other colours. Imagine the surprise then, when Bexleybus, wholly owned by LT, painted buses blue and cream. This colour scheme is seen applied to number 56 (THX239S), a Leyland National, formerly LS239 in the parent fleet. It is seen in Bexleyheath in spring 1988, pursued by a Northern Counties bodied Leyland Olympian in the same livery.

Strange colours also penetrated the very heart of Central London. Grey-Green, a long established North London coach business, had successfully won the contract to operate route 24, a high profile service from Pimlico to Hampstead Heath. Early one morning in March 1989, a London General AEC Routemaster is about to overtake Grey-Green's number 132 (F132PHM) in Trafalgar Square. 132 is a Volvo B10M with Alexander bodywork.

45

Lowland Scottish was formed as part of the preparations for sale of the Scottish Bus Group businesses. It had been split from Eastern Scottish to operate services in the sparsely populated region between Edinburgh and the English border. Berwick-on-Tweed is on that dividing line, just, and it is here that we see open-topper number 1014. This Alexander bodied Daimler Fleetline had been new to Alexander (Fife), registered RXA51J. I found it in the combined Berwick bus station and depot yard in 1989.

Lowland's number 492 (CSG792S) was a Seddon Pennine Mark VII with forty five seat Plaxton Supreme bodywork and was found in the small East Lothian town of Haddington in June 1986. Keeping it company on that day is a similar vehicle in the Eastern Scottish fleet, NSX960T, fleet number YS960W. CSG792S has since been preserved.

New names appeared on the sides of many buses during the 1980s, sometimes as a prelude to the sale of NBC subsidiaries, but others where existing bus companies had expanded into areas beyond their traditional boundaries (see bottom picture). Pilgrim Coaches was an example of the former, born from the splitting up of National Travel West. Here is one of their coaches, number 33 (HBP333X), seen beside Stoke-on-Trent station in spring 1985. The coach body, a Plaxton Supreme, dates from 1981, but the chassis is a 1971 Leyland Leopard, originally registered SHA409K.

Red Admiral was a joint venture between Southampton Citybus and Badgerline, set up to run buses in Portsmouth. However this Iveco 49.10 nineteen seater minibus, registered E953LAE, was photographed in Salisbury in early 1988, in use on a Badgerline service in competition with local operator Wilts and Dorset.

The 'City Clipper' was the name South Yorkshire Transport (formerly SYPTE) gave to its central Sheffield services, where 'bendybuses' took care of the heavy loads. A batch of MAN vehicles was delivered first, but by spring 1981, when this photograph was taken, number 2006 (CRM972T) had been introduced, on loan from British Leyland. It is a Leyland-DAB artic, seating sixty-two with capacity for fifty-eight standees. It is seen in Fitzalan Square, Sheffield, on a decidedly non-springlike day. Several more similar buses were also purchased.

Similar, but later, number 2002 (C102HDT) is seen on 'Clipper' duties outside Sheffield's Pond Street bus station in early 1986, having been delivered in August of the previous year. Sister buses were also used on the former Dearneways service to the Dearne Valley towns.

Pontypridd's buses, previously run by the Urban District Council, had been in the hands of Taff-Ely District Council since 1974. The blue livery always looked smart, as demonstrated by fleet number 24 (RBO24R), a 49 seat Leyland National, seen in Pontypridd town centre on a bright day in 1981.

Taff-Ely normally bought their buses new, but here were a couple of exceptions. These two Leyland PDR1/1 Atlanteans with East Lancs bodywork came second hand from Southampton Citybus. Numbers 81 (TTR161H) and 62 (TTR163H) are seen in the sun at the depot in Treforest in 1984. Taff-Ely sold their operations to National Welsh in 1988.

Takeovers are the subject of this page. The turbulent years of the 1980s saw many smaller operators sell out to their larger neighbours. Somerset operator Brutonian relinquished control of their business to the Cawlett Group (trading as Southern National) in early 1989. Southern National number 2439 (LOD720P) received Brutonian fleetnames and livery. It is a standard Leyland Leopard with Plaxton Supreme coachwork and is seen in Yeovil bus station in September 1989.

Burton's Coaches of Brixham sold out to Devon General in the late 1980s. This 1988 Leyland Tiger/ Plaxton fifty-four seat bus was included in the sale, but was soon transferred to Devon General's sister company, Thames Transit. Still wearing its original owner's identity, it is seen in Oxford's Gloucester Green bus station in late 1989.

Manchester's orange buses were a familiar sight on the city's streets throughout the decade. Even on a dull day, such as this one in mid 1980, the livery offered a bit of brightness to the drab surroundings of Stevenson Square in the city centre, where this MCW Metrobus of Greater Manchester Transport was photographed. Fleet number 5009 (GBU9V) was one of a small batch of such vehicles.

On a much brighter day, in March 1989, orange was still in charge, but changes were afoot. GMT had become Greater Manchester Buses and the smaller lettering 'City South' was a precursor to the splitting up of the company. Number 3282 (F282DRJ), a Leyland Olympian/Northern Counties decker, was photographed in Piccadilly Gardens, central Manchester.

Strathtay Scottish was brought about by splitting off the southern part of Northern Scottish and both vehicles on this page are shown still in the old colours. Fleet number SL34 (JSA105V), 1980 Leyland Leopard with Alexander T type bodywork, is seen in Perth's small bus station in June 1986.

Also photographed in June 1986 was ST11 (B333LSO), this being a Leyland Tiger, again with Alexander coachwork, to the TE design. It is seen in Dundee bus station.

Minibuses were everywhere in the 1980s. A typical Ford Transit is seen here at an unusual location, Ryde Pier Head, where its small size was certainly an advantage. Southern Vectis number 250 (B250LDL) was photographed in late August 1985.

TV Shuttle was a taxi-bus operator, who tried running stage services in the Essex resort of Southend-on-Sea. This Volkswagen minibus, A578XKW, was photographed in the town centre, in spring 1988, dwarfed by the Eastern National Bristol VR behind.

A contrast in coaches from the south west of England. Used on National Express duties was this Volvo B10M/Van Hool 48 seater. Owned by Trathen's of Yelverton (near Plymouth), fleet number A50 (NFJ379W) was photographed in the coach parking area at Battersea in 1982.

The depot of Cornish operator Currian of Nanpean was set amongst the china clay workings, some of which are seen in the left background. The company was the proud owner of this 1968 built Bedford VAM/Plaxton, seen at home in 1982. The history of NRL303F is not known, but the registration indicates that it came from the Bournemouth area.

Kingston-upon-Hull City Transport used the name 'Kingstonian' for the coaching fleet. This is seen applied to number 111 (C111CAT), a Dennis Dominator with coach seated East Lancs bodywork, seen on a rally, about to leave a Hull park for a journey to Bridlington in spring 1986.

Citilink was a mid eighties independent, with services competing with KHCT. Towards the end of the decade, the larger operator had purchased the smaller, but had retained the name and operations. 1970 built Leyland PDR1A/1 WRH281J, with Roe bodywork, formerly in the main KHCT fleet, had received Citilink livery and was photographed in Hull city centre, outside the main depot, summer 1989.

Manchester in the 1980s was a great place for bus enthusiasts! Many new operators had sprung up, such as Citibus of Middleton. A rare vehicle in that company's hands was RTF436L, a former Preston Borough Transport Leyland Panther with Seddon bodywork, never the most popular combination. Built in 1972, it was well past its best when photographed in Piccadilly Gardens bus station, Manchester, in autumn 1986.

At one time, Yelloway was a respected Rochdale coach operator, well known for its long distance express services. Deregulation allowed the company to expand into stage work and a small fleet of second hand double deck buses was obtained for these duties. Seen in Piccadilly Gardens, Manchester in mid 1988, is XRR127M, given fleet number 39. This Bristol VRT/SL6G with ECW bodywork was new to Mansfield District. Passing it is Greater Manchester Transport number 1508 (D506MJA), an Iveco 49.1veco 49.10/Robin Hood 21 seat minibus.

The London to Oxford corridor is, even today, a busy express route. Back in 1980, this Leyland Leopard/Duple Dominant coach was state of the art. It is number 20 (BBW20V) in the City of Oxford fleet and is seen in London's Victoria Coach Station in December 1980.

At the other end of the route, Oxford's Gloucester Green bus station in mid 1987, is City of Oxford number 908 (C908GUD), an MCW Metroliner double deck coach, new in March 1986. Such vehicles were necessary to handle the large numbers of passengers and even today more modern deckers are still in use.

Optare's offering for the 1980s single deck market were the City Pacer and the larger StarRider. M&D Travel had examples of both for use on services around Shrewsbury. Based on the Volkswagen LT55 chassis, this City Pacer had twenty-five seats and is seen in central Shrewsbury in June 1987.

The StarRider used the Mercedes 811D chassis. The type was popular for local services and on these duties is M&D's E402YNT. It is seen in Shrewsbury's old bus station in August 1989. This bus was later repainted into Boulton's of Shropshire livery, as the 'M' in M&D stood for Mick Boulton.

Perthshire is the part of Scotland that gave birth to the mighty Stagecoach empire. A&C McLennan of Spittalfield, later to be taken over by Stagecoach, had a fascinating fleet when I visited in spring 1981. On the right is a former Edinburgh Corporation Leyland PD3/Alexander, registered ASC700B, seen alongside Bedford SB5/Plaxton coach KTS69H, ex Watson of Dundee.

Before the days of Stagecoach as a major player in the UK bus market, a version of the livery is seen on GT Coaches' FGM306D in Perth, also in spring 1981. New to Central SMT as number BL306, it is a Bristol FLF6G with ECW bodywork.

Northern Scottish ordered a large batch of Ford saloons during the 1970s and early 1980s. New in 1979 was number NT194 (FSA194V), a Ford R114/Alexander Y type with 53 bus seats. It was photographed by Richard Huggins outside Peterhead depot on the 14 May 1981.

Another photograph by Richard Huggins, again at Peterhead depot, this time in May 1985. Northern Scottish NCT9A (registered ASA9Y) is a Leyland Tiger with Duple Dominant II coachwork, seen in a Scottish Holidays livery, similar to that used for Citylink express services.

Eastern National's service to central London continued throughout the 1980s. Newly introduced earlier in the year that I captured it on film, fleet number 3073 (KOO791V) was a standard Bristol VRT/ SL3/6LXB with ECW bodywork, specially lettered for the Southend to London Kings Cross service. Surprisingly, normal bus seats were installed, perhaps not the best choice for such a long journey. Kings Cross, September 1980.

By 1985, Eastern National's London service had been upgraded, using Leyland Olympians with ECW double deck coach bodies. Number 4506 (B694BPU) is seen in its 'City Commuter' livery at Southend's Central bus station in spring 1985.

More minibuses in the South West. Somerset operator Henders Coaches of Biddisham were using this ex Midland Fox Ford Transit, B408NJF, on a local service in Bridgwater, September 1989.

An unusual use for this tiny Bedford/Plaxton coach was to transport passengers from Penzance station and town centre to the Heliport, a journey of about a mile. This connected with the unique Isles of Scilly helicopter service operated by British Airways. The bus route was run by a local business, James' Coaches. LAD833E is seen in Penzance in 1982. BA's flights have now ceased, but there are hopes that another company will restore the link.

Sheffield was an interesting place in the eighties, with lots of competition. However, on this page we concentrate on the major operator, South Yorkshire Passenger Transport Executive. The spring of 1981 saw the PTE having a vehicle shortage, so many buses were hired in from a selection of operators. Operating route 52 in the city centre during that period is Leicester City Transport 98 (PBC98G), a 1968 ECW bodied Leyland Atlantean PDR1A/1. The PTE's 239 (HWB239J), a Daimler Fleetline/Park Royal loads up behind.

SYPTE's buses were later renamed as SYT (South Yorkshire's Transport), operating as an 'arm's length' company, in preparation for future privatisation. A wide red band had been added to the old colour scheme, as seen applied to fleet number 2314 (A314XAK), a Northern Counties bodied Dennis Dominator, one of many Guildford build buses in the fleet. It is seen in Sheffield city centre early in 1987..

London Transport's Wandsworth Garage was visited by myself in spring 1988. The depot was being used to house the London Coaches fleet, which contained an interesting collection of non-standard vehicles. Leyland National OJD879R was an exception though, having been transferred from the main fleet, where it was numbered LS79. London Coaches were using it for a schools contract.

Closest to the camera on the same occasion was London Coaches' fleet number LD1 (C766DYO), a Leyland Tiger/Duple Caribbean coach, seen sharing Wandsworth Garage's yard with another Leyland National and an RML type AEC Routemaster used for sightseeing duties.

The preservation movement really took off during the eighties. Two well-presented examples are shown here. West Riding Bedford VAL/Plaxton coach EHL472D is seen lovingly restored to its pre NBC colours, attending a rally in Bridlington in mid 1988.

The Bristol Omnibus Company used 'Bristol Greyhound' as a brand for its coaching business. Restored to this livery is FHW154D, a 1966 Bristol MW6G/ECW 39 seat coach, photographed in Netley Park near Southampton in the summer of 1987.

United Automobile Services had a sizeable fleet of Leyland Nationals. Almost new when photographed in Autumn 1980 was number 3115 (APT115W), a 49 seat example of the Mark 2 version. It is about to leave Bishop Auckland Market Place on route 1 to Darlington.

The latest United livery of the time is applied to an earlier Leyland National, number 3501 (XDL799L), seen in a sunny Whitby bus station in the summer of 1989. The bus was new to Isle of Wight operator Southern Vectis as number 875.

Western National was Cornwall's largest operator. In NBC days, bearing Cornwall Fairways lettering, Leyland National 2846 (PTT85R) is seen in Camborne depot yard in mid 1982.

The new Western National colour scheme is displayed on number 1561 (FDV791V), a 1979 built short Bristol LHS6L/ECW, found on a dull December day outside Truro railway station in 1987. Western National was to be acquired by Badgerline in 1993, later to become part of First Group.

The large Berkshire town of Reading saw major changes in the 1980s. The local NBC operator, Alder Valley, was split into two, with Reading area services being operated under the name of The Bee Line. The yellow livery is seen to good effect on number 504 (CJH125V). This Bristol VRT/SL3/6LXB with ECW body was new to Alder Valley as fleet number 985, originally fitted with coach seating. It is just about to leave the dark depths of Reading bus station in November 1989.

Unlike Alder Valley and The Bee Line, council owned Reading Transport still exists today. Deregulation enabled the undertaking to operate express services to London, for which duties a batch of coach seated Leyland Olympians was ordered. Number 81 (D81UTF) was such a bus, bodied by ECW, and seen outside Reading railway station in November 1985.

The coaching fleet of East Yorkshire Motor Services employed a beautiful blue and primrose colour scheme, until the introduction of standard NBC corporate livery in the early 1970s. The freedoms brought about by the preparations for privatisation brought the colours back to the roads of North Humberside and they are seen to good effect on this Leyland Leopard/Plaxton Supreme Express coach. Number 190 (with cherished registration 8225KH, originally GKH190T) is named 'Holderness Star' and is seen at the main depot on Anlaby Road, Hull in early 1987.

EYMS number 50 (80EYC), named 'Hull Star', is seen in the latest coach livery at Filey in summer 1989. Originally registered B932MLN, it is a 1985 built Volvo B10M-61 with Plaxton Paramount coachwork.

Two variations of the standard London Buses AEC Routemaster are seen on this page. RM90 (VLT90) has lost its roof to become part of the sightseeing fleet and is seen on those duties on the forecourt of Baker Street underground station in June 1987.

The longer version of the Routemaster was known as the RML, but a small batch of these were fitted with platform doors for use on Green Line long distance routes, given the classification of RCL. Along with the Green Line and Country Area services, the RCLs passed to NBC owned London Country, but some were later repurchased to cover for a vehicle shortage. On a foul day in early 1981, RCL2230 (CUV230C) is seen passing Victoria railway station.

United Counties was split into three sections in the 1980s. Prior to that happening, Bristol VRTSL6G/ ECW no 834 (HRP674N) was painted into a version of the original livery to celebrate sixty years of service. I found it in Kettering's bus station in 1982.

United Counties former Luton area operations were later to become Luton and District, but were originally titled Luton Bus. A dark red livery was soon applied, but NBC green was still being carried by number 898 (CBD898T), when photographed in Luton town centre in spring, 1987. It is a Bristol VRT/SL3/6LXB with ECW bus bodywork, new to United Counties in October 1978.

Trials of various types of vehicles were untaken by many companies, using demonstration buses owned by the manufacturers or their agents, sometimes resulting in orders. Not in this case though, as GAC KR type demonstrator C629XEF was the only one of its type to ever run on mainland Britain's roads. Given fleet number 1501, it was used by United Automobile Services for a year, but eventually was sent to join similar buses in the CIE fleet in Eire. I photographed it in Dinsdale, near Darlington, in summer 1986.

On loan to well-known coaching operator Shearings, for its British Coachways operations, was this 1980 built Volvo B58 with the latest style of Plaxton Viewmaster body style. It is seen on a dull day at Kings Cross, London, in early 1981. More details of British Coachways will be revealed later in these pages.

National Express operations in Hanley bus station in the mid 1980s saw a variety of modern coaches in use. Amongst the red buses of PMT and Stoniers is Crosville's B61DMB. Given the fleet number of CBO61, this is a forty-five seat Bova Futura integral, new in April 1985 and photographed in that year.

On the same day, this Leyland Leopard/Duple Dominant 53 seat coach was found departing Hanley for Poole in Dorset. Number 62 (JND262V) in the National Travel West fleet is seen bearing 'Kingfisher' identity, a title that was not to last very long.

Kings Cross coach station was the name given to a spare piece of ground beside London's St Pancras rail terminal. It was originally the site of the Midland Railway's Somers Town goods depot. Later it became a huge hole in the ground, from which rose today's British Library. In the early 1980s, various independent and non National Express or Scottish Citylink express coach services terminated here, benefiting from the recently introduced deregulation of such operations.

British Coachways was a short-lived consortium of well-established companies, including Whittles, Wallace Arnold and Shearings. The latter owned DJA556T (fleet number 308), a 1978 Ford R1114/Plaxton Supreme, fully decked out for such duties, caught on camera at Kings Cross in January 1981.

The rapidly expanding Stagecoach empire had reached London by 1982, with express services from Scotland, using Kings Cross as a terminus. In that year, with St Pancras station as a backdrop, I found Neoplan Skyliner double deck coach LSP223X and more conventional HSP539W, a Duple bodied Volvo B58-61.

North Lincolnshire had a good number of bus operators in the 1980s, by far the largest being Lincolnshire Road Car Company. One of their Bristol VRs is seen in the background, but nearer the camera is YPD114Y, belonging to local independent Daisy of Broughton. This Leyland Tiger/Duple coach had been new to London Country as TD14 and used on Green Line duties. It is seen here outside Scunthorpe bus station in spring 1989.

Council owned operator Grimsby Cleethorpes Transport ran services in the two towns throughout the 1980s, but later sold out to Stagecoach. Demonstrating the latest livery style of the time, June 1983, is number 128 (XFU128V), a Leyland Fleetline/Roe of 1980, seen waiting to depart from Cleethorpes Pier.

Maidstone's buses went far beyond Maidstone! The former Corporation's municipal operations had become Boro'line by the 1980s and this organisation had successfully tendered for several London bus routes. Unsurprisingly, buses had to be brought in a short notice from various sources, one of which was Nottingham City Transport. Still in NCT's green livery, but bearing Boro'line fleetnames, is number 196 PAU196R). Given the name of 'Wilfred', it is a 1976 Daimler Fleetline with Northern Counties bodywork to Nottingham's own specifications. I photographed it beside Waterloo station on route 188 to Greenwich.

Maidstone & District was the name given to the National Bus Company's operations in West Kent and East Sussex. This former BET operator had long owned a fleet that could be said to be standard for an NBC subsidiary, but the chance to buy some second hand Bristol VR types was too good to be missed. Sheffield Corporation Transport had bought a batch of East Lancs bodied examples (VRT/SL6G for the technically minded), but this marque did not find favour with South Yorkshire PTE, who absorbed the municipal operator in 1974. Formerly Sheffield number 287, OWE278K had received fleet number 5778 and NBC green livery when photographed at Hastings depot by the late Les Flint in 1980. A few years later, in preparation for privatisation, M&D's Sussex area operations were separated to become Hastings and District.

The division of Midland Red saw the once huge company split into four new businesses, based on geographical areas, North, South, East and West. Midland Red East became Midland Fox almost immediately, operating in the area around Leicestershire. One of their Leyland Leopard/Marshall dual-purpose saloons, number 345 (GJW45N) is seen in snowy but bright conditions in The Rushes, Loughborough in early 1984.

Midland Red South was given the area around Warwickshire and the South of the West Midlands as their territory. The company also participated in National Express duties to London and here we see fleet number 90 (XCK221R) on such a working. This coach was new to National Travel (West) in 1977 and is a Willowbrook bodied Leyland Leopard, seen at Golders Green bus station in North London, in October 1986. It was common for National Express coaches to stop here at the time, to connect with London Underground tube services into the capital.

South Western Scotland was always an interesting area. This included Ayrshire, where A1 Service ran the very frequent Ardrossan to Kilmarnock route. A1 was a co-operative formed from various small operators based between the two towns. Double decker vehicles predominated, but saloons also put in an appearance, such as Stewart's Leyland Leopard/Duple Dominant fifty-three seat bus OSJ37X. It is seen in the seaside town of Saltcoats in the summer of 1986.

Western Scottish had provided two Fleetlines for my camera at Whitesands, Dumfries, the town's bus terminus by the River Nith, in spring 1981. On the left is Daimler number DR2118 (GCS171E), while the other is a much more modern Leyland version, DR78 (HSD78V). Both carry almost identical Alexander bodywork.

The West Yorkshire Road Car Company had run city services in York for many years, lettering them 'York-West Yorkshire' (in Tilling style, rather than NBC standard font), a reminder of the days of York Corporation trams. Otherwise, normal NBC red is applied to this 1967 built Bristol RELL6G/ECW saloon number 3235 (PYG635E), seen across the road from York's railway station in February 1981.

Just prior to sale of the company to the Blazefield Group, West Yorkshire RCC brought back a version of the old Tilling red livery, demonstrated by these two vehicles inside Bradford Interchange in spring 1987. Number 2571 (KUB545V), on the left, is a Leyland Leopard with Plaxton Supreme coachwork, while standard Leyland Olympian 1837 (A600NYG) is behind.

The Borough of Ipswich ran a fine set of smart green buses throughout the 1980s. The last of a fleet of AECs had vanished by the early part of the decade, leaving Leyland Atlanteans as the oldest buses to be owned. No doubt number 95 (TRT95M) was purchased to replace an AEC Regent III. Seen in the latest colour scheme of the time, it is an AN68/1R with Roe bodywork, photographed at Electric House, the town centre terminus, in 1981.

Number 114 (B114LDX) in the Ipswich fleet was a much rarer bus, though quite the norm in Northern Ireland. Lettered as a Bristol, it was in fact a Leyland B21 with Alexander (Belfast) bodywork. I first assumed that this must have been a diverted order from Ulsterbus, but research has uncovered the fact that it was part of a cancelled batch for Tel Aviv in Israel. Behind the bus is the Town House, a large public house then owned by the local Tolly Cobbold Brewery, seen in spring 1985.

The city of Edinburgh and the Lothians were served by Lothian Regional Transport (formerly Edinburgh Corporation) and several Scottish Bus Group companies during the Eighties. LRT still used the madder and white colour scheme during those years, but black and white paintwork was applied to vehicles with coach seats, such as this otherwise standard Leyland Olympian/Alexander number 371 (F371WSC). It is seen in Edinburgh city centre in summer 1989.

To the west of Edinburgh is the small commuter town of Linlithgow, a historical burgh worth visiting. In the heart of the High Street was the depot of Midland Scottish, where, on a wet summer's day in 1987, I found this fine machine about to go on duty. Number MSE31 (registered FSU320) is a Seddon Pennine/Plaxton Supreme coach, new to Eastern Scottish, but seen here in Midland's Bluebird Coaches livery, looking very smart indeed.

The Mercedes L608D minibus found favour with many operators during the second half of the decade. Here is a typical example, with twenty seat Alexander body in the rather insipid livery of Milton Keynes Citybus (a company formed during the split-up of United Counties). New in October 1986 as number 181 (D181VTP), I found it outside the bus station in MK in spring 1987.

A virtually identical vehicle, albeit with dual-purpose seating, is seen in Doncaster's Northern bus station when new in November 1986. Yorkshire Traction's number 508 (D508NWG) is about to depart for Anchorage Lane, a journey of about a mile and a half. At the wheel is an old friend, Chris Palmer, who is sadly no longer with us.

The capital's Victoria area was used by London Country's Green Line routes as either a terminus or an interchange. By the early 1980s, these services had been upgraded to proper coaches, with Leyland Tigers dominating deliveries. TD10 (YPD110Y) was such a vehicle, with the latest style of Duple Dominant coachwork, seen on Eccleston Bridge (built over Victoria station) in spring 1983.

Another Tiger in the Green Line colours, number TL5 (TPC105X), this time with an ECW coach body, seen sharing Eccleston Bridge with other services some time in 1982. This vehicle had quite a long life, seeing further service with independent operators Davies of Pencader, South Wales and Northern Bus of South Yorkshire.

Council owned bus operations in South Wales were still going strong in the 1980s. Aberdare UDC had become Cynon Valley District Council Transport in the previous decade. Demonstrating the livery adopted by CVDC is Bristol RESL6L/ECW forty-four seat bus number 42 (HTG353N), photographed at the depot in mid 1984. A completely different livery style was later adopted, prior to the sale of the undertaking to Stagecoach.

Very few operators ordered single deck Dennis Dominators, (though Darlington and Hartlepool had some), so it came as rather a surprise to find that Merthyr Tydfil Transport had become the proud owners of number 215 (CKG215V). New in October 1979, it carried fifty seat Marshall bodywork and is seen in Merthyr's bus station when less than a year old.

Transfers between the NBC's coaching fleets for National Express duties were relatively uncommon, but here are a couple. Number 207 (KCK997H) in the National Travel South West stable was a former Ribble Motor Services Leyland Leopard/Plaxton Elite, new in 1970 as Ribble's number 997. I found it in Coventry's Pool Meadow bus station on a sunny day in 1980.

This Greenslades coach was ready for a run to Cheltenham, where (as the destination indicates), connections for much of the National Express network could be made. Greenslades was originally the coaching arm of Devon General and the name had been brought back into use for National Travel South West operations. New to the Bristol Omnibus Company, number 335 (RHY770M), another Plaxton bodied Leopard, is seen in Exeter bus station in March 1981.

Midland Red owned a sizeable fleet of Leyland Nationals, which were distributed to the various constituent concerns when the split-up of the company occurred. Unusually, though, this particular bus was a second hand one, being new to Northern General as number 85L (NCN965L). It is seen here in the hands of Midland Red West as number 165, on a local route in Hereford city centre in mid 1985.

The bright colours of Midland Red West's new livery are seen to good effect in the gloom of the depot-cum-coach station at Digbeth, Birmingham, in November 1986. Again, this a Leyland National transferred from another company. Given number 365 with MRW, it was new as Western National 2801 (GFJ665N).

Red, grey and white was applied in an unusual, but very effective way, as the new livery of Northumbria, formed from the northern section of the United Automobile Company split. The colours look quite snazzy on fleet number 627 (SNU384R), a 1977 built Bristol LH6L/ECW bus, new to Trent Motor Traction. Ashington bus station, August 1988.

Transferred from United was number 226 (RVN248X), a Willowbrook bodied Leyland Leopard, seen on a wonderful August day in 1988, dropping off passengers in Hexham. New in 1982, it had been number 6248 in the United fleet and would have worn the National Bus Company's standard red and white dual-purpose livery.

Crosville in the early 1980s was still one large NBC business, serving North and Central Wales, plus the English county of Cheshire and beyond. Very much a former Tilling company, it had a fleet of standard vehicles. Imagine my surprise then to find this Daimler Fleetline/Northern Counties decker HDL924 (XUF394K) on service in Caernarfon in 1981. It had been purchased a year earlier, from Southdown, where it had been fleet number 394.

NBC dual-purpose livery has been applied to this Crosville coach, along with 'De Cambria' and 'Town Lynx logos, denoting that it has come from the Welsh side of the border. However, it is seen at Chorlton Street, Manchester in 1981, having arrived on an express service. The coach is a Bristol RELH6L with Plaxton Elite Express bodywork.

Kelvin Scottish was a new SBG subsidiary set up in the mid eighties to run services in and around Glasgow, taking over some of the operations of both Midland Scottish and Central SMT. Still in its Midland blue livery is number M47 (BLS425Y), an Alexander bodied MCW Metrobus. I photographed it somewhere in the outskirts of Glasgow in June 1986.

Midland's Kilsyth depot was one of those transferred to Kelvin Scottish and here is one of the buses that came with it. MPE172 (NMS572M) is a Leyland Leopard with classic Alexander Y type bodywork, then still a common sight in Scotland. Kilsyth depot yard, June 1986.

New companies in South West England, as Western National was broken up, included Red Bus (North Devon), running services around the sparsely populated area to the North of Exeter. The largest town in the area is Barnstaple and it is here that we see Red Bus number 2775 (VWR680L), photographed in 1985. This Bristol RELL6G/ECW bus had been new to the West Yorkshire Road Car Company, where it had been numbered 1391.

Another offshoot from Western National was Southern National, bringing back a name from the 1960s and earlier. Their territory was to be Somerset and Dorset. The former is the location here, the busy town of Bridgwater, where, in the summer of 1989, I found this Ford Transit minibus 367 (C929GYD) on town service duties.

Unusual coaches at unusual places could well be the title of this page. Rhymney Valley District Council Transport had been formed in 1974 by the amalgamation of the bus operations of Caerphilly, Gelligaer and Bedwas & Machen Urban District Councils. Apart from visits to Cardiff, their buses were rarely seen outside of the South Wales valleys, so it came as rather a surprise to me to see RVDC's number 28 (C28EUH) passing London's Victoria station in the spring of 1986. New a year earlier, it is a rare Leyland Olympian with coach seated East Lancs bodywork.

The MCW Metroliner coach was never particularly common, but East Kent did own a few. This one, number 8855 (E855UKR), was photographed a long way from home, in Bridlington, East Yorkshire, by Jim Sambrooks in the summer of 1989.

More Ford Transits! This is the last of them in this book, you may be pleased to learn, though I make no apology for showing them, as they really were a feature of the decade. This one, B118RRE, is seen in the hands of Lonsdale Coaches, a subsidiary of Lancaster City Transport. I photographed it in Lancaster's bus station in June 1989.

Even London Transport bought some Transits. FS29 (C501HOE) in the fleet was one of a few that ventured into Hampstead Garden Suburb on the H2 route. Here it is in Golders Green in October 1986.

South Yorkshire PTE had taken over one of Doncaster's famous independent operators, Blue Line/Reliance, in 1979, thereby inheriting the service to Goole via Thorne. Just arrived in Goole, in mid 1980, is Roe bodied Leyland Atlantean AN68A/1R number 1673 (YKY673T), vehicle new to the PTE.

Another independent taken over by SYPTE in 1979 was Severn's of Dunscroft. The depot was included in the purchase and it was where I found number 22 (KWA22W) basking in the sun in 1982. This Leyland National Mark 2 was later fitted with a wheelchair lift.

The North East of England saw an influx of second hand buses, as competition increased in the area. Tyne and Wear PTE, by now trading as Busways, started services outside their normal boundaries, using the fleetname 'Favourite'. Here, in the city of Durham in summer 1988, is number 1807 (KDB677P). New to Greater Manchester Transport, this is a Leyland Leopard with coach seated ECW bodywork.

Another bus that had seen service with Greater Manchester Transport, although it was new to Lancashire United, was Northumbria's 598 (OBN505R). Looking very smart, despite the dull weather in central Newcastle, spring 1987, it was a Daimler Fleetline, bodied by Northern Counties.

Midland Red South operated throughout Warwickshire, after the split-up of its parent company. An unusual purchase for this concern was that of number 957 (YNA329M), a Northern Counties bodied Daimler Fleetline. It had been new to Greater Manchester Transport as number 7374 and was photographed in Leamington Spa in late 1989.

Number 9 in the Midland Red South fleet had been inherited from Midland Red itself, where it had been number 791 (BVP791V). Wearing its new colours, this Leyland Leopard/Willowbrook coach is seen in Warwick town centre in late 1989.

National Express livery is worn by this rare beast of a coach. Used on 'Rapide' duties, Western National's 2352 (AOD645Y) is a Duple bodied Dennis Falcon V, a type that did not find favour with many operators. I found it in London's Victoria Coach Station in 1983.

It is maybe appropriate that the last photograph in this volume was one of the last ones I took in the 1980s. The name Wessex had resurfaced during the decade for National Express coaching operations in the Bristol area. In use on such a duty, heading for London, is this Reeve Burgess bodied Leyland Swift, number 144 (G341VHU), seen in Reading in November 1989.